Hello, mum

Polly Dunbar

faber

First published in 2021
by Faber & Faber Limited
Bloomsbury House
74–77 Great Russell Street
London WC1B 3DA

Printed in Latvia

A CIP record for this book
is available from the British Library

ISBN 978-0-571-36510-4

MIX
Paper from
responsible sources
FSC® C002795
FSC
www.fsc.org

2 4 6 8 10 9 7 5 3 1

For my boys. x

This book came about quite by accident. I've been writing and illustrating books for children since graduating from art school but it wasn't until I had my own children that I thought about drawing something for grown-ups.

I didn't want all those hilarious and beautiful moments of their childhood to float away like wisps on the wind. It seemed the only way to capture them was a quick doodle; a visual diary, if you like. These drawings were mostly made far too early in the morning, coffee in hand, sketchbook on lap, boys clambering over me 'borrowing' my pens.

As well as capturing the sheer exhaustion and utter mayhem of motherhood, I hope I've caught some of the twinkly magic of it all. Children's imaginations have always fascinated me; I guess that's why I write children's books.

I feel very lucky to have my two boys, who show me the world their way, in all its freshness, absurdity and fun.

Thank you to all those who have supported me on social media; it has been hugely encouraging. I'm touched to know that some of you out there relate to these cartoons and feel seen. Of course, thank you to Sonny and Cody, who inspire and wear me out in equal measures - I love you to the kitchen...the moon ...the stars and back again!

Mum, it had better be good.

X

Hello, Baby.

Phase One

How is this possible?

WAAA WAAA WAAA
WAAA WAAA
WAAA
WAAA

How is this possible!?!

This is impossible.

How is this possible?

How are you so impossibly...

... possible.

Phew.

What's that?

Am I enjoying motherhood?

Yes, of course.

FOLD.

Top of the range,
'fold and go.'

just lift...

...and fold

and fold...

...and fold

and told...

and told...

Congratulations!

Folding is complete.

You are good to go!

Oh, you're the loveliest, wuddliest snuggliest, cuddliest thing ever!

What evs.

Growing up, up, up ...

lying

rolling

oh

sitting

oops!

try again...

Crawling

wobbling

walking...

running...

flying...

Phase Two

Jibble wobble
flibble
Cabble dooble
woo.

Abblee
doohee
flooup
floup
pnarrpp.

flibble jib.

Now you're talking.

gluggle
fuggle
sulp

slurp.

Bit tired?

Please sleep.

Mumma...

...Mumma?

Mumma?

Mumma!!!

Mumma.

Dadda!

first we wash...

and then...

we dry.

This is where
I draw the line.

Thanks,

I'm sorry I
lost
my
temper
love.

S'ok
Mumma.

Me time...

You time...

Take home, Mumma?

Take home, Mumma?

Take home, Mumma?

Take home, Mumma

Take
home, Mumma

Gentle.

...Be gentle. Please.

That's not gentle.

No cuddles.

So humiliating.

Somebody... HELP ME!

Oh, hello, baby dinosaur.

carry
carry
carry

wait
wait
wait

got you
got you
got you

please sleep.

Phase Three

Mum?

Mum?

Mum?

Mum?

Mum?

Mum?

Bogey.

Ta, Mum.

I love you all the way
to the kitchen ...

... and back again.

Wow, that's a lot!

And I love you too.

... all the way

to the kitchen...

... and back again.

Mum,
why are
you
crying?

Because
your
shoes
are so
small.

Wow.
Grown-ups
are
weird.

Wee wee, Mum.

my
ball is
too
yucky.

my
ball is
too
Stripy.

My ball is too ball-y.

My
ball
is too ...

...gone.

Poo poo.

where?

Choo
choo
poo
poo

Why?

Why?

Why?

Why?

Why?

Why?

Just...

...because.

Yuck.

Yuck.

ϡ ⊎ ⼂ K.

Yuck.

Y - U - C - K.

Yuck. Yuck. Yuck.

YUCK!!

Yum!

Please
sleep.

Morning!

Too early?

Nah.

Tea, Dad?

There go,

Look, Mum.

Look, Mum.

Wow,

Mum.

poo

poo.

Me keep for ever.

Mum

Mum

Mum

Mum

Mum

Mum   Mum

                    Mum
        Mum

                         Mum

        Mum

                    Mum

        Mum

             Mum

Yes, dear?

This is nice.

Please,

please,

please

sleep.

what's that noise?

Silence?

HE SLEPT!!!

He slept!
He slept!
He slept!

He slept
all night long!

Let's
have
another
one!

Phase Four

Doesn't look
very wonderful
to me.

Meet
your
brother.

It's just
a phase.

Phase Five

Row, Row, Row

your boat

gently down the stream,

merrily, merrily, merrily, merrily,

...life is but a dream.

Let it
all wash
over
you.

Look to the light.

Love.

Live.

Breathe.

Be.

Drink ALL the coffee.

... and if that doesn't work?

Hide.

(somewhere better than this.)

Shall we go home now?

Hey Mom, can't you draw
something funny?

BLAST OFF!!!

1...

2...

3...

Washing the dishes.

Drying the dishes.

Juggling the dishes.

Spinning the dishes.

Dropping the dishes.

Throwing the dishes...

Sweeping the dishes.

Sod the
dishes.

... ordering a takeaway.

Mum, are you
hiding again?

Sleep, please.

My mum!

My mum!

Our mum!

Mum Mum Mum Mum Mum Mum Mum Mum Mum Mum Mum Mum Mum Mum Mum Mum Mum Mum Mum Mum Mum Mum Mum Mum Mum Mum Mum Mum Mum Mum Mum Mum Mum Mum Mum Mum Mum Mum Mum Mum Mum Mum Mum Mum Mum Mum Mum Mum Mum Mum Mum Mum Mum Mum Mum Mum Mum Mum Mum

Mum Mum

Mum

Yes, dears?

Phase Six

There's no loo roll!

Actually...

...don't worry, Mum...

I can reach the curtain...

...All clean now!

I'd give
you the
moon,

I'd give you
the stars,

I'd give you the
whole, wide
world

what's
that?

and all the
beauty in it.

No, I won't give
you a biscuit.

Is anyone going to feed me?

Last time I looked
I was twenty-five.

Maybe if
I just fix
my hair...

... Some earrings....

...A smidge of make-up...

Great.

I've still got it.

I'm
going
out!

Me do it.

One leg...

two legs...

...and pull.

Ta - dah ...

Good to go!

Me time...

You time.

I quite like
this phase.

Don't worry, love.

Nursery will
be great and
you'll be
absolutely
fine.

... absolutely fine.

How was nursery, love?

First I stood like this.

Then I peeped like this.

I was brave and waved like this.

And flapped a bit... like this.

Soon I was flying, like this.

Sounds great!

...And then
what
happened?

This.

Oi, Dad !

Wow, Mum.

Er, Mum.
There's some

IMAGINATION

in the
wash basket...

Phase Seven

and it's looking
at us.

Please put your shoes on.

Put your shoes on.

Are you listening!?

I SAID...

mum! Quick!

Ta.

hhhhhhhh

We're
not going
anywhere until
you're calmed
down.

That's
more
like it.

Now let's
try and have
a nice day.

There
is a
monster.

It is ENORMOUS.

... Has a big
hairy-scary
bum ... like this,

It stomps like
this.

...and when it's
angry..

But that's
ok
'cos everyone
knows...

...even monsters...

... just
need
love.

Bring me
a doughnut.

I
said
doughnut.

where is
my doughnut?

Is anyone even listening?

Does anyone even care...

... about doughnuts?

Giddy-up, horsey!

This phase
is fun.

Look, here comes Archibald...

Hi, Archie!!

He was just a caterpillar.

Look at him now!

Bless.

I'm going to
be a butterfly
when I grow up.

Me too.

Can't you see I'm busy.

...But
Mum!!

The washing is

getting out of hand.

what's up, love?

Tiredy-pops?

Grumpy-wumpy?

Trouser-trouble?

Dinky-winky?

Biccy-wiccy?

cuddle-wuddle-woo-woo?

Mum, do you mind...

I'm just thinking

Sit, Mumma.

Stay.

Fetch,

Mumma.

Good, Mumma.

Lunch?

... Can't you see
we're busy.

I need some
thing.

Tu.

Got any
card board?

Brilliant.

Thanks.

loo rolls?

marvellous

Anything
else
you
need?

Phase Eight

To the moon,
of course!

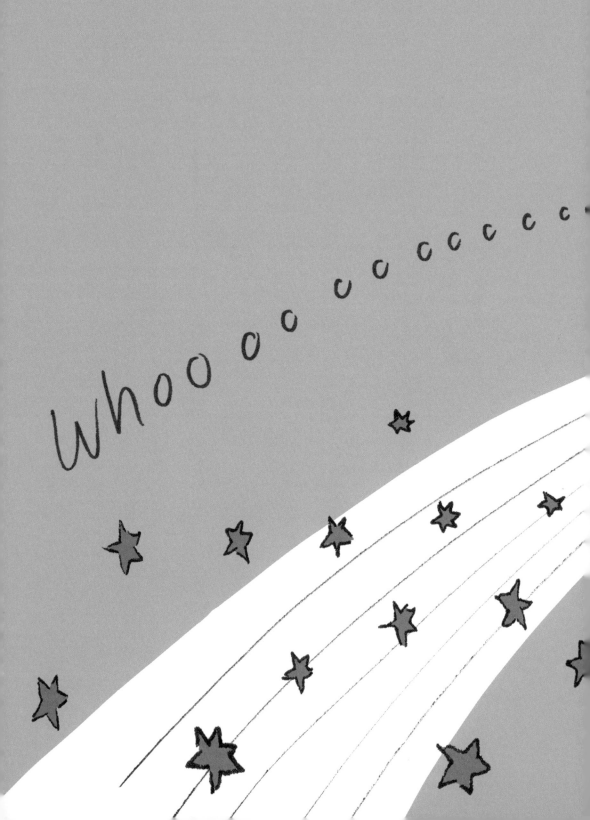

whoo o o o o o o o o o

ok,
Steady
on,
guys.

So, to sum up...

...and a
   magical,
      beautiful
         privilege.

Have you finished
yet, Mum?

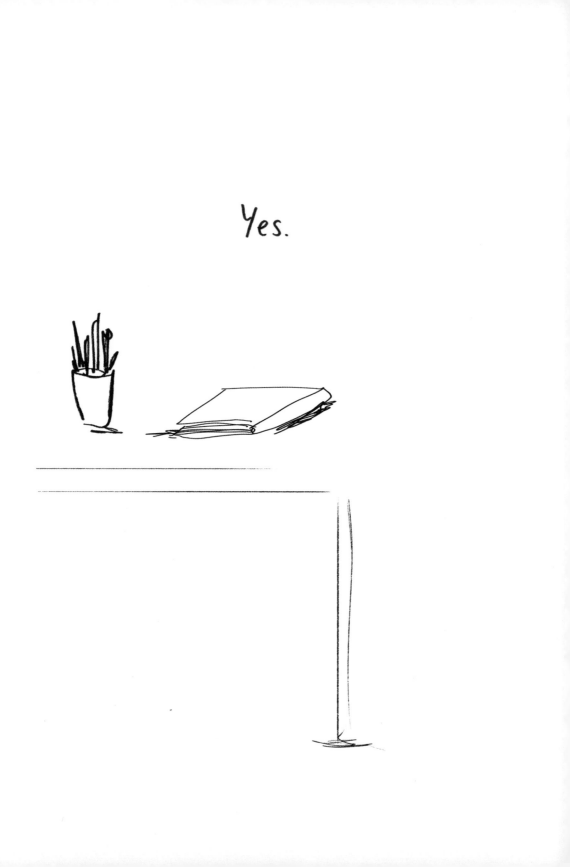

Good.

We need
your
pens.

THe
END